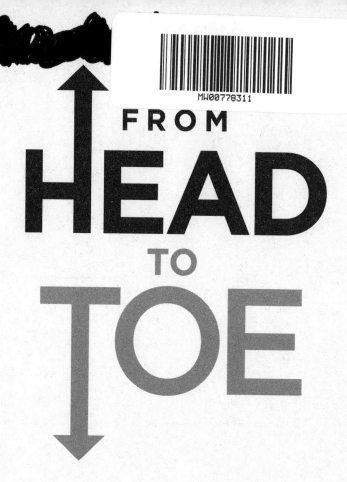

FROM
HEAD
TO
TOE

FROM
HEAD
TO
TOE

JOHN ECKHARDT

FROM HEAD TO TOE by John Eckhardt
Published by John Eckhardt Ministries
PO Box 373
Olympia Fields, IL 60461
www.johneckhardt.global

Unless otherwise noted, all Scripture quotations are taken from the King James Version of the Bible.

Scripture quotations marked AMP are from the Amplified Bible. Copyright © 2015 by The Lockman Foundation. Used by permission. www.Lockman.org

Scripture quotations marked ESV are from the Holy Bible, English Standard Version. Copyright © 2001 by Crossway Bibles, a division of Good News Publishers. Used by permission.

Scripture quotations marked NASB are from the New American Standard Bible, copyright © 1960, 1962, 1963, 1968, 1971, 1972, 1973, 1975, 1977, 1995 by

The Lockman Foundation. Used by permission. www. Lockman.org.

Scripture quotations marked NKJV are taken from the New King James Version®. Copyright © 1982 by Thomas Nelson. Used by permission. All rights reserved.

Scripture quotations marked JUB are taken from the Jubilee Bible, copyright © 2000, 2001, 2010, 2013 by Russell M. Stendal. Used by permission of Russell M. Stendal, Bogota, Colombia. All rights reserved.

Scripture quotations marked MSG are from *The Message: The Bible in Contemporary English*, copyright © 1993, 1994, 1995, 1996, 2000, 2001, 2002. Used by permission of NavPress Publishing Group.

International Standard Book Number: 978-1-62999-721-6
E-book ISBN: 978-1-62999-727-8

19 20 21 22 23 — 987654321
Printed in the United States of America

CONTENTS

PRAYER AND PROPHECY FROM HEAD TO TOE

O my soul, bless GOD. From head to toe,
I'll bless his holy name! O my soul, bless
GOD, don't forget a single blessing!
—PSALM 103:1, MSG

I will praise thee; for I am fearfully and won-
derfully made: marvellous are thy works;
and that my soul knoweth right well.
—PSALM 139:14

THERE IS A verse of Scripture that refers to corruption from the sole of the foot to the top of the head:

From the sole of the foot even unto the head there is no soundness in it; but wounds, and bruises, and putrifying sores: they have not

1

been closed, neither bound up, neither molli-
fied with ointment.

—ISAIAH 1:6

Wounds, bruises, and sores need to be bound up and
healed with ointment. We have foundation to believe that
we are redeemed and healed from head to toe because
of what Jesus accomplished on the cross. He suffered in
His body for our redemption and healing, and we are
healed by His stripes (Isa. 53:5).

- bones pulled out of joint (Ps. 22:14)

- hands and feet pierced (Ps. 22:16)

- beard plucked from His face (Isa. 50:6)

- absolutely marred beyond belief (Isa. 52:14)

- scourged, bruised, and beaten with stripes
  (Matt. 27:26 [cf. furrows—Ps. 129:3]; Isa. 53:5)

- crown of thorns (Matt. 27:29)

- side pierced (John 19:34)

Effectiveness in Prayer and Ministry

Praying and prophesying over someone from head to
toe is an effective way to minister to them in every area.

Praying and prophesying from head to toe covers the person's entire life and body.

This book is the result of a prophetic activation I have done involving prophesying over people from head to toe. Each part of the body is symbolic of something spiritual, and the word of the Lord can bring great blessing, healing, and deliverance. Evil spirits attack and lodge in certain areas, and the word of the Lord can drive them out. We desire to be made whole.

> ...and besought him that they might only touch the hem of his garment: and as many as touched were made perfectly whole.
>
> —MATTHEW 14:36

> And he said unto her, Daughter, thy faith hath made thee whole; go in peace, and be whole of thy plague.
>
> —MARK 5:34

> And whithersoever he entered, into villages, or cities, or country, they laid the sick in the streets, and besought him that they might touch if it were but the border of his garment: and as many as touched him were made whole.
>
> —MARK 6:56

And he said unto her, Daughter, be of good comfort: thy faith hath made thee whole; go in peace.

—LUKE 8:48

When Jesus saw him lie, and knew that he had been now a long time in that case, he saith unto him, Wilt thou be made whole?

—JOHN 5:6

Head— authority and rule, wisdom, knowledge.

CHAPTER 1

PRAYING AND PROPHESYING OVER THE HEAD

THE HEAD REPRESENTS authority and rule. Jesus is the head of the church, the body. The head also represents knowledge, wisdom, the mind, thoughts, and ideas. The gray head represents wisdom. The head can be anointed, lifted, crowned, and covered.

The mind can be renewed, strengthened, spiritual, or carnal. The mind can be at peace or troubled.

We can release the word of the Lord upon the head. It is common to lay hands upon a person's head and prophesy. The following scriptures refer to the head and mind:

> He shall lend to thee, and thou shalt not lend to him: he shall be the head, and thou shalt be the tail.
>
> —DEUTERONOMY 28:44

God, I want to be made whole and healed in my mind. I want my mind to be at peace. In Jesus name. Amen.

And for the precious things of the earth and fulness thereof, and for the good will of him that dwelt in the bush: let the blessing come upon the head of Joseph, and upon the top of the head of him that was separated from his brethren.

—DEUTERONOMY 33:16

And the king loved Esther above all the women, and she obtained grace and favour in his sight more than all the virgins; so that he set the royal crown upon her head, and made her queen instead of Vashti.

—ESTHER 2:17

When his candle shined upon my head, and when by his light I walked through darkness...

—JOB 29:3

But thou, O LORD, art a shield for me; my glory, and the lifter up of mine head.

—PSALM 3:3

Thou hast delivered me from the strivings of the people; and thou hast made me the head of the heathen: a people whom I have not known shall serve me.

—PSALM 18:43

For thou preventest him with the blessings of goodness: thou settest a crown of pure gold on his head.

—PSALM 21:3

Thou preparest a table before me in the presence of mine enemies: thou anointest my head with oil; my cup runneth over.

—PSALM 23:5

And now shall mine head be lifted up above mine enemies round about me: therefore will I offer in his tabernacle sacrifices of joy; I will sing, yea, I will sing praises unto the LORD.

—PSALM 27:6

...who redeemeth thy life from destruction; who crowneth thee with lovingkindness and tender mercies.

—PSALM 103:4

It is like the precious ointment upon the head, that ran down upon the beard, even Aaron's beard: that went down to the skirts of his garments.

—PSALM 133:2

O GOD the Lord, the strength of my salvation, thou hast covered my head in the day of battle.

—PSALM 140:7

For they shall be an ornament of grace unto thy head, and chains about thy neck.

—PROVERBS 1:9

She shall give to thine head an ornament of grace: a crown of glory shall she deliver to thee.

—PROVERBS 4:9

Blessings are upon the head of the just: but violence covereth the mouth of the wicked.

—PROVERBS 10:6

For as he thinketh in his heart, so is he.

—PROVERBS 23:7

His left hand is under my head, and his right hand doth embrace me.

—SONG OF SOLOMON 2:6

I pray that my mind be healed of all disease (mental distress).

Thou wilt keep him in perfect peace, whose mind is stayed on thee: because he trusteth in thee.

—Isaiah 26:3

In that day shall the Lord of hosts be for a crown of glory, and for a diadem of beauty, unto the residue of his people.

—Isaiah 28:5

For they that are after the flesh do mind the things of the flesh; but they that are after the Spirit the things of the Spirit.

—Romans 8:5

For to be carnally minded is death; but to be spiritually minded is life and peace.

—Romans 8:6

And be not conformed to this world: but be ye transformed by the renewing of your mind, that ye may prove what is that good, and acceptable, and perfect, will of God.

—Romans 12:2

…doth not behave itself unseemly, seeketh not her own, is not easily provoked, thinketh no evil.

—1 Corinthians 13:5

God, I want to be healed of the carnal mind and I don't want to think any evil. In Jesus name. Amen.

And be renewed in the spirit of your mind.

—EPHESIANS 4:23

For God hath not given us the spirit of fear; but
of power, and of love, and of a sound mind.

—2 TIMOTHY 1:7

CHAPTER 2

PRAYING AND PROPHESYING OVER THE EYES

THE EYES REPRESENT vision, revelation, and sight. God created the eye to see (both naturally and spiritually). God enlightens the eyes. The eyes can be blessed, opened, or darkened (blinded). Pray for the person's eyes and release the word of the Lord over his eyes and sight.

> The statutes of the LORD are right, rejoicing the heart: the commandment of the LORD is pure, enlightening the eyes.
>
> —PSALM 19:8

> Mine eye also shall see my desire on mine enemies, and mine ears shall hear my desire of the wicked that rise up against me.
>
> —PSALM 92:11

The LORD openeth the eyes of the blind: the LORD raiseth them that are bowed down: the LORD loveth the righteous.

—PSALM 146:8

Let thine eyes look right on, and let thine eyelids look straight before thee.

—PROVERBS 4:25

The hearing ear, and the seeing eye, the LORD hath made even both of them.

—PROVERBS 20:12

He that hath a bountiful eye shall be blessed; for he giveth of his bread to the poor.

—PROVERBS 22:9

For thus hath the LORD said unto me, Go, set a watchman, let him declare what he seeth.

—ISAIAH 21:6

And in that day shall the deaf hear the words of the book, and the eyes of the blind shall see out of obscurity, and out of darkness.

—ISAIAH 29:18

Then the eyes of the blind shall be opened, and the ears of the deaf shall be unstopped.

—ISAIAH 35:5

And the word of the LORD came unto me the second time, saying, What seest thou? And I said, I see a seething pot; and the face thereof is toward the north.

—JEREMIAH 1:13

The light of the body is the eye: if therefore thine eye be single, thy whole body shall be full of light.

—MATTHEW 6:22

But if thine eye be evil, thy whole body shall be full of darkness. If therefore the light that is in thee be darkness, how great is that darkness!

—MATTHEW 6:23

And why beholdest thou the mote that is in thy brother's eye, but considerest not the beam that is in thine own eye?

—MATTHEW 7:3

For this people's heart is waxed gross, and their ears are dull of hearing, and their eyes they have closed; lest at any time they should see with their eyes and hear with their ears, and should understand with their heart, and should be converted, and I should heal them.

—MATTHEW 13:15

But blessed are your eyes, for they see: and your ears, for they hear.

—MATTHEW 13:16

And their eyes were opened, and they knew him; and he vanished out of their sight.

—LUKE 24:31

And immediately there fell from his eyes as it had been scales: and he received sight forthwith, and arose, and was baptized.

—ACTS 9:18

...the eyes of your understanding being enlightened; that ye may know what is the hope of his calling, and what the riches of the glory of his inheritance in the saints.

—EPHESIANS 1:18

CHAPTER 3

PRAYING AND PROPHESYING OVER THE EARS

THE EAR IS connected to hearing God's word and God's voice. Your ears can be opened, blessed, closed, or stopped. Pray for the person's ears and release the word of the Lord over her ears and hearing.

> Doth not the ear try words? and the mouth taste his meat?
>
> —JOB 12:11

> I will incline mine ear to a parable: I will open my dark saying upon the harp.
>
> —PSALM 49:4

> Give ear, O my people, to my law: incline your ears to the words of my mouth.
>
> —PSALM 78:1

Hear me now therefore, O ye children, and depart not from the words of my mouth.

—Proverbs 5:7

Cease, my son, to hear the instruction that causeth to err from the words of knowledge.

—Proverbs 19:27

The hearing ear, and the seeing eye, the Lord hath made even both of them.

—Proverbs 20:12

Bow down thine ear, and hear the words of the wise, and apply thine heart unto my knowledge.

—Proverbs 22:17

Apply thine heart unto instruction, and thine ears to the words of knowledge.

—Proverbs 23:12

Give ye ear, and hear my voice; hearken, and hear my speech.

—Isaiah 28:23

And in that day shall the deaf hear the words of the book, and the eyes of the blind shall see out of obscurity, and out of darkness.

—Isaiah 29:18

And thine ears shall hear a word behind thee, saying, This is the way, walk ye in it, when ye turn to the right hand, and when ye turn to the left.

—Isaiah 30:21

The Lord God hath given me the tongue of the learned, that I should know how to speak a word in season to him that is weary: he wakeneth morning by morning, he wakeneth mine ear to hear as the learned.

—Isaiah 50:4

But they refused to hearken, and pulled away the shoulder, and stopped their ears, that they should not hear.

—Zechariah 7:11

What I tell you in darkness, that speak ye in light: and what ye hear in the ear, that preach ye upon the housetops.

—Matthew 10:27

The blind receive their sight, and the lame walk, the lepers are cleansed, and the deaf hear, the dead are raised up, and the poor have the gospel preached to them.

—Matthew 11:5

He that hath ears to hear, let him hear.

—Matthew 11:15

But blessed are your eyes, for they see: and
your ears, for they hear.

—Matthew 13:16

And he said unto them, Take heed what ye
hear: with what measure ye mete, it shall be
measured to you: and unto you that hear shall
more be given.

—Mark 4:24

And she had a sister called Mary, which also
sat at Jesus' feet, and heard his word.

—Luke 10:39

He that is of God heareth God's words: ye
therefore hear them not, because ye are not of
God.

—John 8:47

How then shall they call on him in whom
they have not believed? and how shall they
believe in him of whom they have not heard?
and how shall they hear without a preacher?

—Romans 10:14

So then faith cometh by hearing, and hearing
by the word of God.

—Romans 10:17

CHAPTER 4

PRAYING AND PROPHESYING OVER THE NOSE

THE NOSE IS connected to smelling and is a symbol of discernment. The nose is what distinguishes odors, scents, and fragrances. The anointing oil was made with spices (perfumed). There is nothing worse than a bad odor. Pray for his nose and smelling and release the word of the Lord. Pray that he would smell the fragrance of Christ.

> And he came near, and kissed him: and he smelled the smell of his raiment, and blessed him, and said, See, the smell of my son is as the smell of a field which the LORD hath blessed.
>
> —GENESIS 27:27

> And Aaron shall burn thereon sweet incense every morning: when he dresseth the lamps, he shall burn incense upon it.
>
> —EXODUS 30:7

And thou shalt make it an oil of holy ointment, an ointment compound after the art of the apothecary: it shall be an holy anointing oil.

—EXODUS 30:25

And thou shalt make it a perfume, a confection after the art of the apothecary, tempered together, pure and holy.

—EXODUS 30:35

Ointment and perfume rejoice the heart: so doth the sweetness of a man's friend by hearty counsel.

—PROVERBS 27:9

Dead flies cause the ointment of the apothecary to send forth a stinking savour: so doth a little folly him that is in reputation for wisdom and honour.

—ECCLESIASTES 10:1

I am the rose of Sharon, and the lily of the valleys.

—SONG OF SOLOMON 2:1

I rose up to open to my beloved; and my hands dropped with myrrh, and my fingers with sweet smelling myrrh, upon the handles of the lock.

—SONG OF SOLOMON 5:5

His cheeks are as a bed of spices, as sweet flowers: his lips like lilies, dropping sweet smelling myrrh.

—SONG OF SOLOMON 5:13

I said, I will go up to the palm tree, I will take hold of the boughs thereof: now also thy breasts shall be as clusters of the vine, and the smell of thy nose like apples.

—SONG OF SOLOMON 7:8

If the whole body were an eye, where were the hearing? If the whole were hearing, where were the smelling?

—1 CORINTHIANS 12:17

For we are unto God a sweet savour of Christ, in them that are saved, and in them that perish.

—2 CORINTHIANS 2:15

But I have all, and abound: I am full, having received of Epaphroditus the things which were sent from you, an odour of a sweet smell, a sacrifice acceptable, wellpleasing to God.

—PHILIPPIANS 4:18

CHAPTER 5

PRAYING AND PROPHESYING
OVER THE MOUTH (VOICE)

THE MOUTH IS for speaking, declaring, decreeing, prophesying, praying, singing, and praising. The mouth includes the tongue and the lips. Pray for the person's mouth and release the word of the Lord over her lips, tongue, and voice.

> And Hannah prayed, and said, My heart rejoiceth in the LORD, mine horn is exalted in the LORD: my mouth is enlarged over mine enemies; because I rejoice in thy salvation.
>
> —1 SAMUEL 2:1
>
> The Spirit of the LORD spake by me, and his word was in my tongue.
>
> —2 SAMUEL 23:2

Thou shalt also decree a thing, and it shall be established unto thee: and the light shall shine upon thy ways.

—JOB 22:28

Out of the mouth of babes and sucklings hast thou ordained strength because of thine enemies, that thou mightest still the enemy and the avenger.

—PSALM 8:2

I will bless the LORD at all times: his praise shall continually be in my mouth.

—PSALM 34:1

And my tongue shall speak of thy righteousness and of thy praise all the day long.

—PSALM 35:28

I said, I will take heed to my ways, that I sin not with my tongue: I will keep my mouth with a bridle, while the wicked is before me.

—PSALM 39:1

And he hath put a new song in my mouth, even praise unto our God: many shall see it, and fear, and shall trust in the LORD.

—PSALM 40:3

My heart is inditing a good matter: I speak of the things which I have made touching the king: my tongue is the pen of a ready writer.

—PSALM 45:1

Hear my voice, O God, in my prayer: preserve my life from fear of the enemy.

—PSALM 64:1

I cried unto God with my voice, even unto God with my voice; and he gave ear unto me.

—PSALM 77:1

For there is not a word in my tongue, but, lo, O LORD, thou knowest it altogether.

—PSALM 139:4

Put away from thee a froward mouth, and perverse lips put far from thee.

—PROVERBS 4:24

He that keepeth his mouth keepeth his life: but he that openeth wide his lips shall have destruction.

—PROVERBS 13:3

Whoso keepeth his mouth and his tongue keepeth his soul from troubles.

—PROVERBS 21:23

And he laid it upon my mouth, and said, Lo, this hath touched thy lips; and thine iniquity is taken away, and thy sin purged.

—Isaiah 6:7

And he hath made my mouth like a sharp sword; in the shadow of his hand hath he hid me, and made me a polished shaft; in his quiver hath he hid me.

—Isaiah 49:2

The Lord God hath given me the tongue of the learned, that I should know how to speak a word in season to him that is weary: he wakeneth morning by morning, he wakeneth mine ear to hear as the learned.

—Isaiah 50:4

I create the fruit of the lips; Peace, peace to him that is far off, and to him that is near, saith the Lord; and I will heal him.

—Isaiah 57:19

Cry aloud, spare not, lift up thy voice like a trumpet, and shew my people their transgression, and the house of Jacob their sins.

—Isaiah 58:1

As for me, this is my covenant with them, saith the LORD; My spirit that is upon thee, and my words which I have put in thy mouth, shall not depart out of thy mouth, nor out of the mouth of thy seed, nor out of the mouth of thy seed's seed, saith the LORD, from henceforth and for ever.

—ISAIAH 59:21

Then the LORD put forth his hand, and touched my mouth. And the LORD said unto me, Behold, I have put my words in thy mouth.

—JEREMIAH 1:9

Not that which goeth into the mouth defileth a man; but that which cometh out of the mouth, this defileth a man.

—MATTHEW 15:11

And these signs shall follow them that believe; in my name shall they cast out devils; they shall speak with new tongues.

—MARK 16:17

As he spake by the mouth of his holy prophets, which have been since the world began.

—LUKE 1:70

For I will give you a mouth and wisdom, which all your adversaries shall not be able to gainsay nor resist.

—LUKE 21:15

Let no corrupt communication proceed out of your mouth, but that which is good to the use of edifying, that it may minister grace unto the hearers.

—EPHESIANS 4:29

And for me, that utterance may be given unto me, that I may open my mouth boldly, to make known the mystery of the gospel.

—EPHESIANS 6:19

By him therefore let us offer the sacrifice of praise to God continually, that is, the fruit of our lips giving thanks to his name.

—HEBREWS 13:15

For he that will love life, and see good days, let him refrain his tongue from evil, and his lips that they speak no guile.

—1 PETER 3:10

CHAPTER 6

PRAYING AND PROPHESYING OVER THE FACE (COUNTENANCE)

THE FACE REPRESENTS your disposition and reveals your inward state. Moses' face shone with glory from being in the presence of God. Your face can be anointed and filled with joy or shame. Pray for the person's face and release the word of the Lord.

> And he washed his face, and went out, and refrained himself, and said, Set on bread.
> —GENESIS 43:31

> And when Aaron and all the children of Israel saw Moses, behold, the skin of his face shone; and they were afraid to come nigh him.
> —EXODUS 34:30

> And he said, Nay; but as captain of the host of the LORD am I now come. And Joshua fell on

his face to the earth, and did worship, and said unto him, What saith my Lord unto his servant?

—JOSHUA 5:14

Wherefore the king said unto me, Why is thy countenance sad, seeing thou art not sick? this is nothing else but sorrow of heart. Then I was very sore afraid.

—NEHEMIAH 2:2

Why art thou cast down, O my soul? and why art thou disquieted within me? hope thou in God: for I shall yet praise him, who is the health of my countenance, and my God.

—PSALM 42:11

Behold, O God our shield, and look upon the face of thine anointed.

—PSALM 84:9

And wine that maketh glad the heart of man, and oil to make his face to shine, and bread which strengtheneth man's heart.

—PSALM 104:15

A merry heart maketh a cheerful countenance: but by sorrow of the heart the spirit is broken.

—PROVERBS 15:13

Iron sharpeneth iron; so a man sharpeneth the countenance of his friend.

—PROVERBS 27:17

His legs are as pillars of marble, set upon sockets of fine gold: his countenance is as Lebanon, excellent as the cedars.

—SONG OF SOLOMON 5:15

Hitherto is the end of the matter. As for me Daniel, my cogitations much troubled me, and my countenance changed in me: but I kept the matter in my heart.

—DANIEL 7:28

Moreover when ye fast, be not, as the hypocrites, of a sad countenance: for they disfigure their faces, that they may appear unto men to fast. Verily I say unto you, They have their reward.

—MATTHEW 6:16

But thou, when thou fastest, anoint thine head, and wash thy face.

—MATTHEW 6:17

... and was transfigured before them: and his face did shine as the sun, and his raiment was white as the light.

—MATTHEW 17:2

And all that sat in the council, looking sted-
fastly on him, saw his face as it had been the
face of an angel.

—ACTS 6:15

And thus are the secrets of his heart made
manifest; and so falling down on his face he
will worship God, and report that God is in
you of a truth.

—1 CORINTHIANS 14:25

But we all, with open face beholding as in a
glass the glory of the Lord, are changed into
the same image from glory to glory, even as by
the Spirit of the Lord.

—2 CORINTHIANS 3:18

For ye suffer, if a man bring you into bondage,
if a man devour you, if a man take of you, if
a man exalt himself, if a man smite you on
the face.

—2 CORINTHIANS 11:20

Having many things to write unto you, I would
not write with paper and ink: but I trust to
come unto you, and speak face to face, that our
joy may be full.

—2 JOHN 12

CHAPTER 7

PRAYING AND PROPHESYING OVER THE NECK

THE NECK CAN have ornaments of grace and beauty or be under a yoke of bondage. Stubbornness is also connected with the neck. The neck also includes the throat.

> And Pharaoh took off his ring from his hand, and put it upon Joseph's hand, and arrayed him in vestures of fine linen, and put a gold chain about his neck.
>
> —GENESIS 41:42

> Judah, thou art he whom thy brethren shall praise: thy hand shall be in the neck of thine enemies; thy father's children shall bow down before thee.
>
> —GENESIS 49:8

Thou hast also given me the necks of mine enemies; that I might destroy them that hate me.

—PSALM 18:40

Lift not up your horn on high: speak not with
a stiff neck.

—PSALM 75:5

For they shall be an ornament of grace unto
thy head, and chains about thy neck.

—PROVERBS 1:9

Let not mercy and truth forsake thee: bind
them about thy neck; write them upon the
table of thine heart.

—PROVERBS 3:3

So shall they be life unto thy soul, and grace
to thy neck.

—PROVERBS 3:22

Bind them continually upon thine heart, and
tie them about thy neck.

—PROVERBS 6:21

And put a knife to thy throat, if thou be a man
given to appetite.

—PROVERBS 23:2

He, that being often reproved hardeneth his neck, shall suddenly be destroyed, and that without remedy.

—Proverbs 29:1

Thy neck is like the tower of David builded for an armoury, whereon there hang a thousand bucklers, all shields of mighty men.

—Song of Solomon 4:4

Thy neck is as a tower of ivory; thine eyes like the fishpools in Heshbon, by the gate of Bathrabbim: thy nose is as the tower of Lebanon which looketh toward Damascus.

—Song of Solomon 7:4

And it shall come to pass in that day, that his burden shall be taken away from off thy shoulder, and his yoke from off thy neck, and the yoke shall be destroyed because of the anointing.

—Isaiah 10:27

Shake thyself from the dust; arise, and sit down, O Jerusalem: loose thyself from the bands of thy neck, O captive daughter of Zion.

—Isaiah 52:2

For it shall come to pass in that day, saith the Lord of hosts, that I will break his yoke from off thy neck, and will burst thy bonds, and strangers shall no more serve themselves of him.

—JEREMIAH 30:8

Our necks are under persecution: we labour, and have no rest.

—LAMENTATIONS 5:5

I decked thee also with ornaments, and I put bracelets upon thy hands, and a chain on thy neck.

—EZEKIEL 16:11

Then commanded Belshazzar, and they clothed Daniel with scarlet, and put a chain of gold about his neck, and made a proclamation concerning him, that he should be the third ruler in the kingdom.

—DANIEL 5:29

Their throat is an open sepulchre; with their tongues they have used deceit; the poison of asps is under their lips.

—ROMANS 3:13

...who have for my life laid down their own necks: unto whom not only I give thanks, but also all the churches of the Gentiles.

—ROMANS 16:4

CHAPTER 8

PRAYING AND PROPHESYING OVER THE SHOULDERS

PROPHETICALLY THE SHOULDERS represent burden bearing or the weight of responsibility. You may have heard the saying, "They are walking around as if they are carrying the weight of the world on their shoulders." When we see people consumed or oppressed by the spirit of heaviness, sometimes it manifests in slumped shoulders or as a bent-over posture. Insecurity or self-consciousness can also be discerned by the position of one's shoulders.

On the other hand, upright shoulders represent confidence. When a person walks tall with his shoulders back and head up, we get the sense of strength, poise in handling difficult circumstances, assurance, and positive self-esteem.

The shoulders also represent government (Isa. 9:6).

And he saw that rest was good, and the land that it was pleasant; and bowed his shoulder to bear, and became a servant unto tribute.

—GENESIS 49:15

And Samson lay till midnight, and arose at midnight, and took the doors of the gate of the city, and the two posts, and went away with them, bar and all, and put them upon his shoulders, and carried them up to the top of an hill that is before Hebron.

—JUDGES 16:3

And the children of the Levites bare the ark of God upon their shoulders with the staves thereon, as Moses commanded according to the word of the LORD.

—1 CHRONICLES 15:15

I removed his shoulder from the burden: his hands were delivered from the pots.

—PSALM 81:6

For thou hast broken the yoke of his burden, and the staff of his shoulder, the rod of his oppressor, as in the day of Midian.

—ISAIAH 9:4

For unto us a child is born, unto us a son is given: and the government shall be upon his shoulder: and his name shall be called Wonderful, Counsellor, The mighty God, The everlasting Father, The Prince of Peace.

—Isaiah 9:6

And it shall come to pass in that day, that his burden shall be taken away from off thy shoulder, and his yoke from off thy neck, and the yoke shall be destroyed because of the anointing.

—Isaiah 10:27

I will break the Assyrian in my land, and upon my mountains tread him under foot: then shall his yoke depart from off them, and his burden depart from off their shoulders.

—Isaiah 14:25

Thus saith the Lord GOD, Behold, I will lift up mine hand to the Gentiles, and set up my standard to the people: and they shall bring thy sons in their arms, and thy daughters shall be carried upon their shoulders.

—Isaiah 49:22

But they refused to hearken, and pulled away the shoulder, and stopped their ears, that they should not hear.

—ZECHARIAH 7:11

For they bind heavy burdens and grievous to be borne, and lay them on men's shoulders; but they themselves will not move them with one of their fingers.

—MATTHEW 23:4

CHAPTER 9

PRAYING AND PROPHESYING
OVER THE BACK

THE BACK SUPPORTS the body. A strong back represents power and strength. A bent-over back represents oppression and bondage. The back also represents what is behind a person or what is hidden. Stripes on the back represent correction.

> The plowers plowed upon my back: they made long their furrows.
>
> —PSALM 129:3
>
> In the lips of him that hath understanding wisdom is found: but a rod is for the back of him that is void of understanding.
>
> —PROVERBS 10:13
>
> Judgments are prepared for scorners, and stripes for the back of fools.
>
> —PROVERBS 19:29

The north wind driveth away rain: so doth an angry countenance a backbiting tongue.

—PROVERBS 25:23

A whip for the horse, a bridle for the ass, and a rod for the fool's back.

—PROVERBS 26:3

I gave my back to the smiters, and my cheeks to them that plucked off the hair: I hid not my face from shame and spitting.

—ISAIAH 50:6

Then shall thy light break forth as the morning, and thine health shall spring forth speedily: and thy righteousness shall go before thee; the glory of the LORD shall be thy reward.

—ISAIAH 58:8

CHAPTER 10

PRAYING AND PROPHESYING OVER THE LUNGS (BREATH)

THE LUNGS ARE connected to breathing. Breathing is connected to life. Breath is wind and air. These are also pictures of the Holy Spirit. Pray for the person's lungs and breathing and release the word of the Lord.

> And the LORD God formed man of the dust of the ground, and breathed into his nostrils the breath of life; and man became a living soul.
>
> —GENESIS 2:7

> But God clave an hollow place that was in the jaw, and there came water thereout; and when he had drunk, his spirit came again, and he revived: wherefore he called the name thereof Enhakkore, which is in Lehi unto this day.
>
> —JUDGES 15:19

In whose hand is the soul of every living thing, and the breath of all mankind.

—JOB 12:10

All the while my breath is in me, and the spirit of God is in my nostrils.

—JOB 27:3

Let every thing that hath breath praise the LORD. Praise ye the LORD.

—PSALM 150:6

Thus saith God the LORD, he that created the heavens, and stretched them out; he that spread forth the earth, and that which cometh out of it; he that giveth breath unto the people upon it, and spirit to them that walk therein...

—ISAIAH 42:5

Thou hast heard my voice: hide not thine ear at my breathing, at my cry.

—LAMENTATIONS 3:56

And I will lay sinews upon you, and will bring up flesh upon you, and cover you with skin, and put breath in you, and ye shall live; and ye shall know that I am the LORD.

—EZEKIEL 37:6

So I prophesied as he commanded me, and the breath came into them, and they lived, and stood up upon their feet, an exceeding great army.

—EZEKIEL 37:10

And when he had said this, he breathed on them, and saith unto them, Receive ye the Holy Ghost.

—JOHN 20:22

...neither is worshipped with men's hands, as though he needed any thing, seeing he giveth to all life, and breath, and all things.

—ACTS 17:25

CHAPTER 11

PRAYING AND PROPHESYING OVER THE HEART

THE HEART REPRESENTS the inward man, the spirit. The heart can be merry, pure, large, wise, broken, hardened, and wicked. God gives the believer a new heart. Lay your hands on the person's heart and pray for her. Release the word of the Lord over her heart.

> And God gave Solomon wisdom and understanding exceeding much, and largeness of heart, even as the sand that is on the sea shore.
>
> —1 KINGS 4:29
>
> Create in me a clean heart, O God; and renew a right spirit within me.
>
> —PSALM 51:10

The sacrifices of God are a broken spirit: a broken and a contrite heart, O God, thou wilt not despise.

—PSALM 51:17

Thy word have I hid in mine heart, that I might not sin against thee.

—PSALM 119:11

He healeth the broken in heart, and bindeth up their wounds.

—PSALM 147:3

Trust in the LORD with all thine heart; and lean not unto thine own understanding.

—PROVERBS 3:5

Keep thy heart with all diligence; for out of it are the issues of life.

—PROVERBS 4:23

Hope deferred maketh the heart sick: but when the desire cometh, it is a tree of life.

—PROVERBS 13:12

A sound heart is the life of the flesh: but envy the rottenness of the bones.

—PROVERBS 14:30

A merry heart maketh a cheerful countenance: but by sorrow of the heart the spirit is broken.

—PROVERBS 15:13

A man's heart deviseth his way: but the LORD directeth his steps.

—PROVERBS 16:9

A merry heart doeth good like a medicine: but a broken spirit drieth the bones.

—PROVERBS 17:22

Before destruction the heart of man is haughty, and before honour is humility.

—PROVERBS 18:12

The Spirit of the Lord GOD is upon me; because the LORD hath anointed me to preach good tidings unto the meek; he hath sent me to bind up the brokenhearted, to proclaim liberty to the captives, and the opening of the prison to them that are bound.

—ISAIAH 61:1

A new heart also will I give you, and a new spirit will I put within you: and I will take away the stony heart out of your flesh, and I will give you an heart of flesh.

—EZEKIEL 36:26

Blessed are the pure in heart: for they shall see God.

—MATTHEW 5:8

For where your treasure is, there will your heart be also.

—MATTHEW 6:21

A good man out of the good treasure of the heart bringeth forth good things: and an evil man out of the evil treasure bringeth forth evil things.

—MATTHEW 12:35

So likewise shall my heavenly Father do also unto you, if ye from your hearts forgive not every one his brother their trespasses.

—MATTHEW 18:35

But after thy hardness and impenitent heart treasurest up unto thyself wrath against the day of wrath and revelation of the righteous judgment of God.

—ROMANS 2:5

But let it be the hidden man of the heart, in that which is not corruptible, even the ornament of a meek and quiet spirit, which is in the sight of God of great price.

—1 PETER 3:4

CHAPTER 12

PRAYING AND PROPHESYING OVER THE BELLY (STOMACH, BOWELS)

THE STOMACH (BELLY) represents the inward part of man. The belly is also connected to conceiving and birthing. The stomach is also connected to the bowels.

In figurative language, the bowels (intestines) "denote deep emotions of various kinds. As in physiology we speak of the 'nervus sympathicus,' the ancients expressed by these terms 'affection,' 'sympathy,' and 'mercy,' feelings of distress and sorrow, as in Job 30:27 the King James Version; Lamentations 1:20 the King James Version; Lamentations 2:11 the King James Version. In one passage we have to translate me`im by 'heart,' being the seat of affection and devotion (Psalm 71:6): 'Thy law is within my heart' (Psalm 40:8). In the New Testament (Revised Version) the word is only given in Acts 1:18."[1]

Pray for the person's stomach and release the word of the Lord over his belly.

> He hath swallowed down riches, and he shall vomit them up again: God shall cast them out of his belly.
>
> —JOB 20:15

> Behold, my belly is as wine which hath no vent; it is ready to burst like new bottles. I will speak, that I may be refreshed: I will open my lips and answer.
>
> —JOB 32:19–20

> Have mercy upon me, O LORD, for I am in trouble: mine eye is consumed with grief, yea, my soul and my belly.
>
> —PSALM 31:9

> For our soul is bowed down to the dust: our belly cleaveth unto the earth.
>
> —PSALM 44:25

> It shall be health to thy navel, and marrow to thy bones.
>
> —PROVERBS 3:8

The words of a talebearer are as wounds, and they go down into the innermost parts of the belly.

—PROVERBS 18:8

A man's belly shall be satisfied with the fruit of his mouth; and with the increase of his lips shall he be filled.

—PROVERBS 18:20

The spirit of man is the candle of the LORD, searching all the inward parts of the belly.

—PROVERBS 20:27

Before I formed thee in the belly I knew thee; and before thou camest forth out of the womb I sanctified thee, and I ordained thee a prophet unto the nations.

—JEREMIAH 1:5

And as for thy nativity, in the day thou wast born thy navel was not cut, neither wast thou washed in water to supple thee; thou wast not salted at all, nor swaddled at all.

—EZEKIEL 16:4

And said, I cried by reason of mine affliction unto the LORD, and he heard me; out of the belly of hell cried I, and thou heardest my voice.

—JONAH 2:2

When I heard, my belly trembled; my lips quivered at the voice: rottenness entered into my bones, and I trembled in myself, that I might rest in the day of trouble: when he cometh up unto the people, he will invade them with his troops.

—HABAKKUK 3:16

He that believeth on me, as the scripture hath said, out of his belly shall flow rivers of living water.

—JOHN 7:38

God, I pray that my belly be healed (my inner parts) of all sickness and disease. I pray that out of my belly shall flow rivers of living waters. I will be made whole and healed of all distress. In Jesus name. Amen.

CHAPTER 13

PRAYING AND PROPHESYING OVER THE KIDNEYS AND LIVER (REINS, INWARD PARTS)

*R*EINS IS THE Hebrew word *kilyah* meaning "a kidney (as an essential organ); figuratively, the mind (as the interior self)—kidneys, reins."[1] "The liver and kidneys [are] vital internal organs of the body Pr 7:23. See also Job 16:13; 20:24–25. The liver and kidneys are symbolic of human emotions and the conscience Ps 73:21. The Hebrew words for liver and kidneys are occasionally translated as 'heart,' 'spirit' or 'inmost being.' See also Job 19:27; Pr 23:16; Jer 12:2; La 2:11; 3:13."[2] The liver signifies interior purification because it purifies the blood. The kidneys represent the inward parts, the internal organs. Pray for the person's inward parts (kidneys and liver) and release the word of the Lord.

> For thou hast possessed my kidneys: thou
> hast covered me in my mother's womb.
>
> —PSALM 139:13, JUB

"The kidneys owe their importance in the Bible partly to the fact that they are imbedded in fat, and fat of such purity that fat of the kidneys was a proverbial term for surpassing excellence."[3]

"In the books of the Bible that follow the Pentateuch, mostly in Jeremiah and Psalms, the human kidneys are cited figuratively as the site of temperament, emotions, prudence, vigor, and wisdom. In five instances, they are mentioned as the organs examined by God to judge an individual."[4]

"The position of the kidneys in the body makes them particularly inaccessible, and in cutting up an animal they are the last organs to be reached. Consequently, they were a natural symbol for the most hidden part of a man (Psalm 139:13), and in Job 16:13 to 'cleave the reins asunder' is to effect the total destruction of the individual (compare Job 19:27; Lamentations 3:13). This hidden location, coupled with the sacred sacrificial use, caused the kidneys to be thought of as the seat of the innermost moral (and emotional) impulses. So the reins instruct (Psalm 16:7) or are 'pricked' (Psalm 73:21), and God can be said to be far from the reins of sinners (Jeremiah 12:2)."[5]

> And he took all the fat that was upon the inwards, and the caul above the liver, and the two kidneys, and their fat, and Moses burned it upon the altar.
>
> —LEVITICUS 8:16

> His arrows surround me. Without mercy He splits my kidneys open; He pours out my gall on the ground.
>
> —JOB 16:13, NASB

> His arrows surround me. He pierces my kidneys (vital organs) without mercy; He pours out my gall on the ground.
>
> —JOB 16:13, AMP

> I will bless the LORD, who hath given me counsel: my reins also instruct me in the night seasons.
>
> —PSALM 16:7

> Examine me, O LORD, and prove me; try my reins and my heart.
>
> —PSALM 26:2

Behold, thou desirest truth in the inward parts: and in the hidden part thou shalt make me to know wisdom.

—PSALM 51:6

Thus my heart was grieved, and I was pricked in my reins.

—PSALM 73:21

For thou hast possessed my reins: thou hast covered me in my mother's womb.

—PSALM 139:13

Till a dart strike through his liver; as a bird hasteth to the snare, and knoweth not that it is for his life.

—PROVERBS 7:23

Yea, my reins shall rejoice, when thy lips speak right things.

—PROVERBS 23:16

My beloved put in his hand by the hole of the door, and my bowels were moved for him.

—SONG OF SOLOMON 5:4

I the LORD search the heart, I try the reins, even to give every man according to his ways, and according to the fruit of his doings.

—JEREMIAH 17:10

Behold, O LORD; for I am in distress: my bowels are troubled; mine heart is turned within me; for I have grievously rebelled: abroad the sword bereaveth, at home there is as death.

—LAMENTATIONS 1:20

Mine eyes do fail with tears, my bowels are troubled, my liver is poured upon the earth, for the destruction of the daughter of my people; because the children and the sucklings swoon in the streets of the city.

—LAMENTATIONS 2:11

He hath caused the arrows of his quiver to enter into my reins.

—LAMENTATIONS 3:13

He drove into my kidneys the arrows of his quiver.

—LAMENTATIONS 3:13, ESV

For God is my record, how greatly I long after you all in the bowels of Jesus Christ.

—PHILIPPIANS 1:8

If there be therefore any consolation in Christ, if any comfort of love, if any fellowship of the Spirit, if any bowels and mercies...

—PHILIPPIANS 2:1

But whoso hath this world's good, and seeth his brother have need, and shutteth up his bowels of compassion from him, how dwelleth the love of God in him?

—1 JOHN 3:17

And I will kill her children with death; and all the churches shall know that I am he which searcheth the reins and hearts: and I will give unto every one of you according to your works.

—REVELATION 2:23

CHAPTER 14

PRAYING AND PROPHESYING OVER THE HANDS

HANDS REPRESENT WORSHIP (lifting the hands), warfare (as in Psalm 144:1, "the LORD... teacheth my hands to war, and my fingers to fight"), labor (the work of your hands), serving, and helping. Hands can be anointed for healing and prosperity. They also represent holding on or letting go.

Pray for the person's hands and release the word of the Lord over her hands.

> The LORD rewarded me according to my righteousness; according to the cleanness of my hands hath he recompensed me.
>
> —PSALM 18:20

> He teacheth my hands to war, so that a bow of steel is broken by mine arms.
>
> —PSALM 18:34

He that hath clean hands, and a pure heart; who hath not lifted up his soul unto vanity, nor sworn deceitfully.

—PSALM 24:4

Hear the voice of my supplications, when I cry unto thee, when I lift up my hands toward thy holy oracle.

—PSALM 28:2

O clap your hands, all ye people; shout unto God with the voice of triumph.

—PSALM 47:1

Thus will I bless thee while I live: I will lift up my hands in thy name.

—PSALM 63:4

The desire of the slothful killeth him; for his hands refuse to labour.

—PROVERBS 21:25

Give her of the fruit of her hands; and let her own works praise her in the gates.

—PROVERBS 31:31

Better is an handful with quietness, than both the hands full with travail and vexation of spirit.

—ECCLESIASTES 4:6

By much slothfulness the building decayeth; and through idleness of the hands the house droppeth through.

—ECCLESIASTES 10:18

Thus saith the LORD to his anointed, to Cyrus, whose right hand I have holden, to subdue nations before him; and I will loose the loins of kings, to open before him the two leaved gates; and the gates shall not be shut.

—ISAIAH 45:1

They shall not build, and another inhabit; they shall not plant, and another eat: for as the days of a tree are the days of my people, and mine elect shall long enjoy the work of their hands.

—ISAIAH 65:22

The hands of Zerubbabel have laid the foundation of this house; his hands shall also finish it; and thou shalt know that the LORD of hosts hath sent me unto you.

—ZECHARIAH 4:9

And if thy hand offend thee, cut it off: it is better for thee to enter into life maimed, than having two hands to go into hell, into the fire that never shall be quenched.

—MARK 9:43

They shall take up serpents; and if they drink any deadly thing, it shall not hurt them; they shall lay hands on the sick, and they shall recover.

—MARK 16:18

Then laid they their hands on them, and they received the Holy Ghost.

—ACTS 8:17

And, behold, the angel of the Lord came upon him, and a light shined in the prison: and he smote Peter on the side, and raised him up, saying, Arise up quickly. And his chains fell off from his hands.

—ACTS 12:7

And God wrought special miracles by the hands of Paul.

—ACTS 19:11

Let him that stole steal no more: but rather let him labour, working with his hands the thing which is good, that he may have to give to him that needeth.

—EPHESIANS 4:28

And that ye study to be quiet, and to do your own business, and to work with your own hands, as we commanded you.

—1 THESSALONIANS 4:11

I will therefore that men pray every where, lifting up holy hands, without wrath and doubting.

—1 TIMOTHY 2:8

Neglect not the gift that is in thee, which was given thee by prophecy, with the laying on of the hands of the presbytery.

—1 TIMOTHY 4:14

Lay hands suddenly on no man, neither be partaker of other men's sins: keep thyself pure.

—1 TIMOTHY 5:22

Wherefore I put thee in remembrance that thou stir up the gift of God, which is in thee by the putting on of my hands.

—2 TIMOTHY 1:6

Draw nigh to God, and he will draw nigh to you. Cleanse your hands, ye sinners; and purify your hearts, ye double minded.

—JAMES 4:8

CHAPTER 15

PRAYING AND PROPHESYING OVER THE ARMS

A RMS ARE A symbol of strength, protection, caring, and blessing. Jesus blessed the children by taking them into His arms. Pray for the person's arms and release the word of the Lord.

> But his bow abode in strength, and the arms of his hands were made strong by the hands of the mighty God of Jacob; (from thence is the shepherd, the stone of Israel).
>
> —GENESIS 49:24

> The eternal God is thy refuge, and underneath are the everlasting arms: and he shall thrust out the enemy from before thee; and shall say, Destroy them.
>
> —DEUTERONOMY 33:27

And when he came unto Lehi, the Philistines shouted against him: and the Spirit of the LORD came mightily upon him, and the cords that were upon his arms became as flax that was burnt with fire, and his bands loosed from off his hands.

—JUDGES 15:14

Delilah therefore took new ropes, and bound him therewith, and said unto him, The Philistines be upon thee, Samson. And there were liers in wait abiding in the chamber. And he brake them from off his arms like a thread.

—JUDGES 16:12

He teacheth my hands to war, so that a bow of steel is broken by mine arms.

—PSALM 18:34

For the arms of the wicked shall be broken: but the LORD upholdeth the righteous.

—PSALM 37:17

She girdeth her loins with strength, and strengtheneth her arms.

—PROVERBS 31:17

And he took a child, and set him in the midst of them: and when he had taken him in his arms, he said unto them, Whosoever shall receive one of these little children in my name receiveth me.

—MARK 9:36

And he took them up in his arms, put his hands upon them, and blessed them.

—MARK 10:16

And he came by the Spirit into the temple: and when the parents brought in the child Jesus, to do for him after the custom of the law, then took he him up in his arms, and blessed God, and said, Lord, now lettest thou thy servant depart in peace, according to thy word.

—LUKE 2:27–29

CHAPTER 16

PRAYING AND PROPHESYING OVER THE BONES

HEALTHY BONES AND marrow are important to good health. Marrow produces the blood, which is necessary for a strong immune system. Your bones can be dry (unhealthy) or moist (healthy). The bones provide structure for the body and make up the skeletal system. Dry bones are symbolic of death. Marrow is a picture of fatness and prosperity. As you pray and prophesy over a person's bones, pray for his bones *and* marrow. Then release the word of the Lord.

> Have mercy upon me, O LORD; for I am weak:
> O LORD, heal me; for my bones are vexed.
>
> —PSALM 6:2

> He keepeth all his bones: not one of them is broken.
>
> —PSALM 34:20

All my bones shall say, LORD, who is like unto thee, which deliverest the poor from him that is too strong for him, yea, the poor and the needy from him that spoileth him?

—PSALM 35:10

Make me to hear joy and gladness; that the bones which thou hast broken may rejoice.

—PSALM 51:8

My soul shall be satisfied as with marrow and fatness; and my mouth shall praise thee with joyful lips.

—PSALM 63:5

Be not wise in thine own eyes: fear the LORD, and depart from evil. It shall be health to thy navel, and marrow to thy bones.

—PROVERBS 3:7–8

A sound heart is the life of the flesh: but envy the rottenness of the bones.

—PROVERBS 14:30

The light of the eyes rejoiceth the heart: and a good report maketh the bones fat.

—PROVERBS 15:30

Pleasant words are as an honeycomb, sweet to the soul, and health to the bones.

—PROVERBS 16:24

A merry heart doeth good like a medicine: but a broken spirit drieth the bones.

—PROVERBS 17:22

And in this mountain shall the LORD of hosts make unto all people a feast of fat things, a feast of wines on the lees, of fat things full of marrow, of wines on the lees well refined.

—ISAIAH 25:6

And the LORD shall guide thee continually, and satisfy thy soul in drought, and make fat thy bones: and thou shalt be like a watered garden, and like a spring of water, whose waters fail not.

—ISAIAH 58:11

And when ye see this, your heart shall rejoice, and your bones shall flourish like an herb: and the hand of the LORD shall be known toward his servants, and his indignation toward his enemies.

—ISAIAH 66:14

Then I said, I will not make mention of him, nor speak any more in his name. But his word was in mine heart as a burning fire shut up in my bones, and I was weary with forbearing, and I could not stay.

—JEREMIAH 20:9

And he said unto me, Son of man, can these bones live? And I answered, O Lord GOD, thou knowest. Again he said unto me, Prophesy upon these bones, and say unto them, O ye dry bones, hear the word of the LORD.

—EZEKIEL 37:3–4

Thus saith the Lord GOD unto these bones; Behold, I will cause breath to enter into you, and ye shall live.

—EZEKIEL 37:5

So I prophesied as I was commanded: and as I prophesied, there was a noise, and behold a shaking, and the bones came together, bone to his bone.

—EZEKIEL 37:7

For the word of God is quick, and powerful, and sharper than any twoedged sword, piercing even to the dividing asunder of soul and spirit,

and of the joints and marrow, and is a discerner
of the thoughts and intents of the heart.

—HEBREWS 4:12

CHAPTER 17

PRAYING AND PROPHESYING OVER THE KNEES

KNEES ARE CONNECTED to prayer and worship. Strong knees represent prayer and worship. Weak knees represent discouragement. God commands us to strengthen the feeble knees. Kneeling is a sign of submission and humility. Pray for the person's knees and release the word of the Lord over her knees.

> Thy words have upholden him that was falling, and thou hast strengthened the feeble knees.
>
> —JOB 4:4

> O come, let us worship and bow down: let us kneel before the LORD our maker.
>
> —PSALM 95:6

> My knees are weak through fasting; and my flesh faileth of fatness.
>
> —PSALM 109:24

Strengthen ye the weak hands, and confirm the feeble knees.

—ISAIAH 35:3

Again he measured a thousand, and brought me through the waters; the waters were to the knees. Again he measured a thousand, and brought me through; the waters were to the loins.

—EZEKIEL 47:4

And he was withdrawn from them about a stone's cast, and kneeled down, and prayed.

—LUKE 22:41

And when he had thus spoken, he kneeled down, and prayed with them all.

—ACTS 20:36

For it is written, As I live, saith the Lord, every knee shall bow to me, and every tongue shall confess to God.

—ROMANS 14:11

For this cause I bow my knees unto the Father of our Lord Jesus Christ.

—EPHESIANS 3:14

Wherefore lift up the hands which hang down, and the feeble knees.

—HEBREWS 12:12

CHAPTER 18

PRAYING AND PROPHESYING
OVER THE FEET

FEET ARE CONNECTED to your walk and your path. Those who proclaim the gospel have beautiful feet. Feet are also connected to dancing and leaping. Pray for the person's feet and release the word of the Lord over his feet.

> Every place whereon the soles of your feet shall tread shall be yours: from the wilderness and Lebanon, from the river, the river Euphrates, even unto the uttermost sea shall your coast be.
>
> —DEUTERONOMY 11:24

> He maketh my feet like hinds' feet, and setteth me upon my high places.
>
> —PSALM 18:33

Thou hast enlarged my steps under me, that my feet did not slip.

—PSALM 18:36

I have wounded them that they were not able to rise: they are fallen under my feet.

—PSALM 18:38

Mine eyes are ever toward the LORD; for he shall pluck my feet out of the net.

—PSALM 25:15

Thou hast turned for me my mourning into dancing: thou hast put off my sackcloth, and girded me with gladness.

—PSALM 30:11

...and hast not shut me up into the hand of the enemy: thou hast set my feet in a large room.

—PSALM 31:8

The law of his God is in his heart; none of his steps shall slide.

—PSALM 37:31

He brought me up also out of an horrible pit, out of the miry clay, and set my feet upon a rock, and established my goings.

—PSALM 40:2

Thou shalt tread upon the lion and adder: the young lion and the dragon shalt thou trample under feet.

—PSALM 91:13

Thy word is a lamp unto my feet, and a light unto my path.

—PSALM 119:105

Ponder the path of thy feet, and let all thy ways be established.

—PROVERBS 4:26

How beautiful upon the mountains are the feet of him that bringeth good tidings, that publisheth peace; that bringeth good tidings of good, that publisheth salvation; that saith unto Zion, Thy God reigneth!

—ISAIAH 52:7

The sons also of them that afflicted thee shall come bending unto thee; and all they that despised thee shall bow themselves down at the soles of thy feet; and they shall call thee; The city of the LORD, The Zion of the Holy One of Israel.

—ISAIAH 60:14

The LORD God is my strength, and he will make my feet like hinds' feet, and he will make me to walk upon mine high places. To the chief singer on my stringed instruments.

—HABAKKUK 3:19

And ye shall tread down the wicked; for they shall be ashes under the soles of your feet in the day that I shall do this, saith the LORD of hosts.

—MALACHI 4:3

Behold, I give unto you power to tread on serpents and scorpions, and over all the power of the enemy: and nothing shall by any means hurt you.

—LUKE 10:19

And he leaping up stood, and walked, and entered with them into the temple, walking, and leaping, and praising God.

—ACTS 3:8

And make straight paths for your feet, lest that which is lame be turned out of the way; but let it rather be healed.

—HEBREWS 12:13

CHAPTER 19

DECLARATIONS FOR HEALING, DELIVERANCE, AND BLESSINGS FROM HEAD TO TOE

HEALING, DELIVERANCE, AND the blessing of God are part of God's covenant. As we remain in covenant with God, we can pray and speak these declarations in faith, believing that we have all that God has promised us.

Deliverance From Head to Toe

I command any evil spirits operating in my head or against my mind to leave in the name of Jesus.

I command any evil spirits operating in my eyes and sight to leave.

I command any evil spirits operating in my ears and hearing to leave.

I command any evil spirits operating in my mouth and tongue to leave.

I command any evil spirits operating in my neck and throat to leave.

I command any evil spirits operating in my chest and lungs to leave.

I command any evil spirits operating in my shoulders, spine, and back to leave.

I command all evil spirits operating in my heart to leave.

I command all evil spirits operating in my stomach to leave.

I command all evil spirits operating in my kidneys and liver to leave.

I command all evil spirits operating in my spleen and pancreas to leave.

I command all evil spirits operating in my glands to leave.

I command all evil spirits operating in my sexual organs to leave.

I command all evil spirits operating in my bones and skeletal system to leave.

I command all evil spirits operating in my nervous system to leave.

I command all evil spirits operating in my circulatory system to leave.

I command all evil spirits operating in my arms, hands, legs, and feet to leave.

Blessed From Head to Toe

I am blessed from head to toe.

Blessings are upon my head.

My mind is blessed.

My thoughts are blessed.

My ideas are blessed.

My eyes are blessed.

My ears are blessed.

My mouth and tongue are blessed.

My neck and throat are blessed.

My lungs and breathing are blessed.

My shoulders are blessed.

My hands are blessed.

My back and spine are blessed.

My heart is blessed.

My stomach and bowels are blessed.

My navel is blessed.

My kidneys, liver, and inward parts are blessed.

My loins are blessed.

My knees are blessed.

My feet are blessed.

My bones and marrow are blessed.

Anointed From Head to Toe

And of Asher he said, Let Asher be blessed with children; let him be acceptable to his brethren, and let him dip his foot in oil.

—Deuteronomy 33:24

Thou preparest a table before me in the presence of mine enemies: thou anointest my head with oil; my cup runneth over.

—Psalm 23:5

> It is like the precious ointment upon the head, that ran down upon the beard, even Aaron's beard: that went down to the skirts of his garments.
>
> —PSALM 133:2

Let the anointing flow from the top of my head to the soles of my feet.

Let my head be anointed with fresh oil.

Let my mind be anointed to think correctly.

Let my ears be anointed to hear Your voice and Your word.

Let my eyes be anointed to see.

Let my eyes be anointed for revelation.

Let my mouth and tongue be anointed to prophesy, preach, declare, and decree Your word.

Let my tongue be anointed to sing the new song.

Let my hands be anointed for healing and prosperity.

Let my hands be anointed for war.

Let my hands be anointed to heal the sick.

Let my hands be anointed to cast out demons.

Let my hands be anointed to write.

Let my feet be anointed to walk in the paths of righteousness.

Let my feet be anointed to tread on serpents and scorpions.

Cleansed From Head to Toe

> He that hath clean hands, and a pure heart; who hath not lifted up his soul unto vanity, nor sworn deceitfully.
>
> —PSALM 24:4

> Wash me thoroughly from mine iniquity, and cleanse me from my sin.
>
> —PSALM 51:2

> Purge me with hyssop, and I shall be clean: wash me, and I shall be whiter than snow.
>
> —PSALM 51:7

> Let us draw near with a true heart in full assurance of faith, having our hearts sprinkled from an evil conscience, and our bodies washed with pure water.
>
> —HEBREWS 10:22

Let me be cleansed "with the washing of water by the word" (Eph. 5:26).

Let my mind and thoughts be cleansed.

Let my mouth and tongue be purged and cleansed.

Let no unclean words come out of my mouth.

Let my heart be clean.

Let all unforgiveness and bitterness be cleansed from my heart.

Let me have clean hands.

Lord, cleanse my inward parts.

Let me be cleansed from head to toe.

Let all impurity be cleansed from my life.

Let my feet and my path be clean.

Let me have clean relationships.

Let me be cleansed from any unclean spirits in any part of my life or body.

Favor From Head to Toe

Let favor be upon my life from head to toe.

Let favor rest upon my head.

Let me have favored thoughts and ideas.

Let favor be seen in my face.

Let my ears be favored to hear good things.

Let my eyes be favored to see great things.

Let my eyes be favored to see the mysteries of God.

Let my mouth and tongue be favored to speak great things.

Let my shoulders be favored to carry the burden of the Lord.

Let my neck have a chain of favor and grace.

Let my back be favored and strong.

Let my arms be favored and strong.

Let favor rest in my heart.

Let my bones be favored and rejoice.

Let my hands be favored and prosper.

Let my knees be favored to pray and worship.

Let my feet experience favor.

Let me walk in the path of favor.

Let favor surround me like a shield.

Prayer of Submission From Head to Toe

I beseech you therefore, brethren, by the mercies of God, that ye present your bodies a living sacrifice, holy, acceptable unto God, which is your reasonable service.

—Romans 12:1

Submit yourselves therefore to God. Resist the devil, and he will flee from you.

—James 4:7

I submit my entire body from head to toe as a living sacrifice.

I submit my head, mind, and thoughts to the Lord.

I submit my ears to the Lord.

I submit my eyes and vision to the Lord.

I submit my nose to the Lord.

I submit by mouth, lips, and tongue to the Lord.

I submit my neck and shoulders to the Lord.

I submit my back to the Lord.

I submit my chest, breathing, and lungs to the Lord.

I submit my heart to the Lord.

I submit my stomach, appetite, and belly to the Lord.

I submit my kidneys and liver (inward parts) to the Lord.

I submit my hands to the Lord.

I submit my knees to the Lord.

I submit my feet and walk to the Lord.

Restoration From Head to Toe

> And I will restore to you the years that the locust hath eaten, the cankerworm, and the caterpiller, and the palmerworm, my great army which I sent among you.
>
> —JOEL 2:25

I receive restoration from head to toe of anything stolen from me by the enemy.

I receive restoration for my head and my thoughts.

I receive restoration for my ears and hearing.

I receive restoration for my eyes, vision, and seeing.

I receive restoration for my mouth and tongue.

I receive restoration for my neck and shoulders.

I receive restoration for my chest and breathing.

I receive restoration for by heart.

I receive restoration for my hands.

I receive restoration for my stomach, bowels, and belly.

I receive restoration for my bones.

I receive restoration for my knees.

I receive restoration for my feet.

Protected and Covered From Head to Toe

Keep me as the apple of the eye, hide me under the shadow of thy wings.

—Psalm 17:8

He that dwelleth in the secret place of the most High shall abide under the shadow of the Almighty.

—Psalm 91:1

Shield

But thou, O Lord, art a shield for me; my glory, and the lifter up of mine head.

—Psalm 3:3

Thou hast also given me the shield of thy salvation: and thy right hand hath holden me up, and thy gentleness hath made me great.

—PSALM 18:35

The LORD is my strength and my shield; my heart trusted in him, and I am helped: therefore my heart greatly rejoiceth; and with my song will I praise him.

—PSALM 28:7

Our soul waiteth for the LORD: he is our help and our shield.

—PSALM 33:20

Above all, taking the shield of faith, wherewith ye shall be able to quench all the fiery darts of the wicked.

—EPHESIANS 6:16

Helmet (head)

O GOD the Lord, the strength of my salvation, thou hast covered my head in the day of battle.

—PSALM 140:7

And take the helmet of salvation, and the sword of the Spirit, which is the word of God.

—EPHESIANS 6:17

But let us, who are of the day, be sober, putting on the breastplate of faith and love; and for an helmet, the hope of salvation.

—1 THESSALONIANS 5:8

Breastplate (chest, heart)

Stand therefore, having your loins girt about with truth, and having on the breastplate of righteousness.

—EPHESIANS 6:14

Feet

They shall bear thee up in their hands, lest thou dash thy foot against a stone.

—PSALM 91:12

...and your feet shod with the preparation of the gospel of peace.

—EPHESIANS 6:15

Back

Then shall thy light break forth as the morning, and thine health shall spring forth speedily;

and thy righteousness shall go before thee; the glory of the LORD shall be thy reward.

—Isaiah 58:8

CHAPTER 20

PRAYING FOR YOUR PASTOR AND LEADERS FROM HEAD TO TOE

THOSE WHO LEAD in the kingdom and even those who have authority in the marketplace need prayer for the weight of responsibility they carry. Paul said in 1 Timothy 2:1–2, "Therefore I exhort first of all that supplications, prayers, intercessions, and giving of thanks be made for all men, for kings and all who are in authority, that we may lead a quiet and peaceable life in all godliness and reverence" (NKJV).

Use these declarations to pray and prophesy peace, blessing, wisdom, and increase over the leaders in your life.

Let my pastor and leaders be anointed with fresh oil.

Let my pastor and leaders be anointed from the top of the head to the soles of the feet.

Let my pastor and leaders be crowned with wisdom and honor.

Let my pastor and leaders think clearly and accurately.

Let my pastor and leaders have the mind of Christ.

Let my pastor and leaders have the spirit of knowledge, wisdom, and understanding.

Let my pastor's and leaders' thoughts be established according to the Lord's will.

Let my pastor's and leaders' eyes be anointed to see.

Let the glory of God be in my pastor's and leaders' faces.

Let my pastor and leaders hear the voice of the Lord clearly.

Let my pastor's and leaders' ears be opened to the sounds of heaven.

Let my pastor and leaders discern between good and evil.

Let my pastor's and leaders' mouths be anointed to speak the word of the Lord.

Let my pastor's and leaders' mouths be anointed to preach, teach, and prophesy.

Let my pastor and leaders speak the truth in love.

Let my pastor and leaders boldly proclaim the truth.

Let my pastor preach the good news to the poor and needy.

Let my pastor's and leaders' shoulders be strong to govern and rule.

Let my pastor's and leaders' necks have the ornament of grace and favor.

Let my pastor's and leaders' back be protected from all hidden attacks.

Let rivers of living water flow from my pastor's belly.

Breathe the breath of life on my pastor and leaders.

Let my pastor and leaders walk in integrity and pureness of heart.

Let my pastor's and leaders' hands be anointed for healing, deliverance, and miracles.

Let my pastor's and leaders' hands be anointed to prosper.

Let pastor's and leaders' knees be strengthened for worship and prayer.

Let my pastor and leaders walk in the way of righteousness.

Let my pastor and leaders walk in the path of truth.

NOTES

Chapter 12
Praying and Prophesying Over the Belly (Stomach, Bowels)

1. Bible Hub, s.v. "bowels," accessed May 10, 2019, http://
   bibleencyclopedia.com/bowels.htm.

Chapter 13
Praying and Prophesying Over the Kidneys
and Liver (Reins, Inward Parts)

1. Bible Hub, s.v. "*kilyah*," accessed May 10, 2019, https://
   biblehub.com/hebrew/3629.htm.
2. Martin H. Manser, Alister E. McGrath, J. I. Packer, Donald
   J. Wiseman, eds., *The Complete Topical Guide to the Bible*
   (Grand Rapids, MI: Baker Books, 2017).
3. Bible Hub, s.v. "kidneys," accessed May 11, 2019, http://
   biblehub.com/topical/k/kidneys.htm.
4. Garabed Eknoyan, "The Kidneys in the Bible: What
   Happened?," *Journal of American Society of Nephrology* 16, no.
   12 (December 2005): 3464–3471, https://doi.org/10.1681/
   ASN.2005091007.
5. Bible Hub, s.v. "kidneys."